PRAYERSCRIPTS
Speaking God's Word Back to Him

STANDING IN THE GAP *for*

NATIONAL

HEALING

★ ★ ★ ★ ★

40 *Days of Prayer for*

★ RECONCILIATION ★ RIGHTEOUSNESS ★ RESTORATION ★

CYRIL OPOKU

Standing in the Gap for National Healing: 40 Days of Prayer for Reconciliation, Righteousness, and Restoration

© 2025 Cyril Opoku. *PrayerScripts*. All rights reserved.

Published by *Quest Publications*

ISBN: 978-1-988439-62-4

Cover design by *Quest Publications (questpublications@outlook.com)*

Unless otherwise indicated, all Scripture quotations are taken from the World English Bible (WEB), which is in the public domain. For more information, visit: www.worldenglish.bible

This book is a work of devotional encouragement. It is not intended to replace biblical study, pastoral counsel, or professional therapy.

Printed in the United States of America.

First Edition: July 2025

For more books like this, visit *PrayerScripts:* https://prayerscripts.org

CONTENTS

PREFACE

There comes a moment in every generation when God calls His people to rise—not in protest, not in pride, but in prayer. I believe this is such a moment.

Standing in the Gap for National Healing: 40 Days of Prayer for Reconciliation, Righteousness, and Restoration was birthed out of a burden—a holy ache—for our nation to return to God. As division deepens, truth bends, and foundations shake, intercessors must take their place on the walls. We are not helpless bystanders in the face of national unrest; we are God's ambassadors, called to partner with Him through intercession for His will to be done on earth as it is in heaven.

This book is an invitation to those who believe that prayer still changes things. That God still hears. That healing is possible. Over 40 days, we will journey together through the brokenness of our land and lift up prayers rooted in Scripture—prayers of repentance, reconciliation, truth, justice, restoration, and hope.

Each prayer is a cry from the heart, guided by the Word, shaped by the Spirit, and aimed at the throne of God. Whether you are praying alone, with a small group, or across a congregation, my hope is that these prayers will ignite a deeper hunger for revival and a stronger resolve to stand in the gap for the nation we love.

May the Lord hear from heaven. May He forgive. May He heal our land.

For His glory alone,
Cyril O.
Illinois, July 2025

INTRODUCTION

Healing doesn't begin in the headlines.
It begins in the hearts of God's people.

All around us, we see the signs of a nation in distress—division, violence, corruption, confusion, and a growing hunger for something real, something true. Yet throughout history, God has always responded to a remnant who would humble themselves, seek His face, and pray. When the people of God stand in the gap, God moves.

Standing in the Gap for National Healing: 40 Days of Prayer for Reconciliation, Righteousness, and Restoration is more than a devotional—it's a call to intercession. It's an invitation to take up your spiritual assignment and cry out to the Lord on behalf of your city, your leaders, your community, and your country.

This book is divided into three sections:

- **Peace, Unity & Reconciliation** – where we begin with the heart of God for healing fractured relationships and restoring unity across races, families, and generations.

- **Morality, Truth & Righteous Leadership** – where we plead for a return to integrity, justice, and godly leadership in every sphere of influence.

- **National Restoration & Reformation** – where we ask God to rebuild what's been torn down, revive what's grown cold, and lead us into a new day of righteousness and purpose.

Each day offers a focused theme, a Scripture-based prayer, and a powerful opportunity to align with God's redemptive plan for our land.

You don't have to be a pastor or prophet to pray. You just need a willing heart, a surrendered spirit, and a vision for what could be if we let God have His way.

Whether you're standing in the gap as a parent, a student, a leader, or a lone voice in the wilderness—your prayers matter. Heaven is listening.

Let us not grow weary. Let us not lose heart. Let us stand—together—for the healing of our nation.

Why "National Healing"?

The phrase *"national healing"* may sound political to some, but in truth, it's deeply biblical. In **2 Chronicles 7:14**, God gives a timeless promise to His people: *"If My people, who are called by My name, will humble themselves and pray and seek My face and turn from their wicked ways, then I will hear from heaven, and I will forgive their sin and heal their land."* Healing begins not with governments, policies, or movements, but with God's people responding to His call. It is a spiritual restoration that comes when hearts are softened, sin is confessed, and a nation bows before the One who made it.

When we speak of "national healing," we are not asking for surface-level peace or temporary relief from crisis—we are crying out for a deep, holy transformation that touches the soul of a nation. It's about more than unity; it's about repentance. It's about turning from wickedness and returning to the Lord. Only then can the spiritual, moral, and even physical land be healed. God has not abandoned His desire to restore; He is still searching for those willing to stand in the gap, seek His face, and believe that His promise still stands.

"Standing in the Gap"

When Ezekiel recorded God's lament—*"I looked for someone among them who would build up the wall and stand in the gap before Me on behalf of the land"* (Ezekiel 22:30)—he captured the very essence of intercession. To "stand in the gap" is to place yourself between a broken people and a holy God, pleading for mercy, justice, and restoration. This book equips you to take that posture daily.

What You Can Expect

1. **Biblical Foundations:** Every prayer in this book is built on the unshakable truth of God's Word. Scripture is not used as a decoration—it is the foundation, the fuel, and the framework for every intercession. As you pray through the passages, you'll find yourself aligned with God's heart and anchored in His promises. You won't be praying opinions or emotions; you'll be declaring the Word of the Lord over your nation.

2. **Focused Themes:** Each day targets a specific area of national need—peace, justice, unity, leadership, repentance, and restoration. These themes are organized to walk you through a spiritual progression from brokenness to healing. The structure is intentional, guiding you to intercede with clarity and purpose as you cover every dimension of your nation's spiritual life.

3. **Honest, Intercessory Prayer:** This isn't surface-level prayer. It's deep, honest, and raw—reflecting the heart of an intercessor who stands in the gap, weeps between the porch and the altar, and refuses to let go until God answers. These prayers express both sorrow and hope, repentance and bold faith. They invite

you to be vulnerable before God while standing boldly on behalf of your land.

4. **Faith for Transformation** – This book is not just about praying for change—it's about believing God can change things. As you pray, expect your faith to grow. Expect your vision to enlarge. Expect to see glimpses of renewal—in your own heart, your community, and even the headlines. We serve a God who still heals nations. Let every prayer be a declaration that transformation is not only possible—it's already beginning.

A Word About Authority and Honor

Intercessors sometimes wrestle with frustration toward leaders or systems. This guide intentionally cultivates a posture of honor—not excusing injustice, but praying from a place of respect for God-ordained authority (Romans 13:1). Change that flows from honor carries heaven's fragrance; criticism birthed in bitterness rarely bears righteous fruit.

Invitation to Partnership

This book is not an end in itself; it is a tool for partnership. Pair it with fasting. Gather a few friends on a video call. Print the daily Scriptures and post them in your workplace. Use it as a 40-day sprint, a weekly prayer rhythm, or a small-group study. The design is modular so churches, prayer groups, and individuals can adapt it to their context. Ask your pastor if your church can spend a month in focused national intercession. God loves to answer united, scriptural prayer.

Final Charge

As you embark on this 40-day journey, don't underestimate the power of your prayers. You are not just reading words on a page—you are standing in the gap, partnering with heaven, and declaring God's purposes over a nation in need. This is holy work. Stay faithful, stay focused, and stay expectant. Let your voice rise like incense before the throne, knowing that the God who hears is also the God who heals. May you be strengthened for the days ahead, bold in your intercession, and unwavering in your faith. Now, take your place on the wall—your nation needs your prayers.

How to Use This Book

This book is designed to be a 40-day prayer journey of intercession for national healing, based on God's Word and guided by the Holy Spirit. Whether you are praying individually, with a small group, or leading a church-wide initiative, here's how to make the most of each day's entry:

1. Set Aside a Daily Time for Prayer

Consistency matters. Choose a quiet time each day to focus, pray, and reflect. Mornings are ideal for many, but any time of day that allows you to pray without distraction will work.

2. Read the Daily Theme and Scripture

Each day includes a clear theme that targets a specific area of need in the nation. Read the accompanying Scripture slowly and prayerfully. Let the Word speak to your spirit before you begin to pray.

3. Pray the Written Prayer Aloud or Silently

The prayers provided are deeply rooted in Scripture and crafted to express the heart of an intercessor. Pray them aloud or in silence—either way, let the words become your own as you lift them before God with faith and sincerity.

4. Add Your Own Intercession

Use the written prayers as a launching pad for your own intercession. Name your city, your leaders, your concerns. Let the Spirit lead you to pray beyond the page. Feel free to journal what the Lord shows you during your time in prayer.

5. Gather Others to Pray with You

Though you can use this book alone, it becomes even more powerful when used in unity with others. Consider inviting friends, family, or your church to take the 40-day journey together. You may even want to host weekly gatherings or online prayer check-ins.

6. Believe and Expect Results

This isn't a religious exercise—it's a faith-filled mission. As you pray, expect God to move. Watch for changes, both spiritual and tangible. Remember, God is listening, and He is faithful to His Word.

Let this be more than a devotional. Let it be a holy assignment. You are standing in the gap for a nation under God—and your prayers are making a difference.

SECTION 1:
PEACE, UNITY & RECONCILIATION

Before a nation can be healed, it must be reconciled—first to God, then to one another. Division is one of the enemy's oldest strategies, and we see the evidence all around us: racial tensions, political hostility, fractured families, and spiritual disunity. But God's Word calls His people to be peacemakers, bridge-builders, and agents of reconciliation. His heart has never changed—He still desires *"to make peace through the blood of His cross"* (Colossians 1:20) and to unite us as one people under His rule.

This first section of prayer focuses on the deep, spiritual work of peace and unity. These are not passive words—they are spiritual battlegrounds. We begin by seeking the peace of our cities, crying out for racial and generational healing, and repenting for the pride and division that have hardened hearts. We pray for the Church to walk in oneness, for mercy to triumph over judgment, and for the bonds of peace to replace walls of hostility. As you intercede, ask God to start this work in your heart and extend it outward—until reconciliation becomes a national reality, not just a spiritual ideal. Let the healing begin with peace.

Day 1: SEEK THE PEACE OF THE CITY

Seek the peace of the city where I have caused you to be carried
away captive, and pray to Yahweh for it; for in its peace you will
have peace."
—Jeremiah 29:7 WEB

O Sovereign Lord, God of Heaven and Earth, You who rule over nations
and set kings in their place, we come before You today as intercessors—
standing in the gap for a nation longing for healing, for unity, and for
Your peace.

You said through Your prophet, *"Seek the peace and prosperity of the city
to which I have carried you... Pray to the Lord for it, because if it prospers,
you too will prosper"* (Jeremiah 29:7). So, Lord, we seek the peace of this
land. Not a peace built by the hands of men, but a peace born from
righteousness, forged in truth, and secured by Your Spirit.

Father, we confess that division has pierced the soul of our nation. Walls
have been raised between brother and brother, tribe and tribe, race and
race, party and party. But You, O Lord, are the God who tears down
walls. You are our Peace, who has broken down every dividing wall of
hostility. We ask You to do it again. Break every yoke of offense. Silence
every voice that foments hate. Heal the generational wounds that bleed
beneath the surface. Pour the oil of reconciliation where there has been
bitterness, suspicion, and betrayal.

We pray for the cities and regions You have placed us in—not with
condemnation, but with compassion. Let every neighborhood, every
rural town, every urban center come under the canopy of Your
presence. Send revival to city halls and street corners, to school boards

and sanctuaries. Let peace flow like a river through the places where chaos and confusion have reigned.

God of mercy, teach us to pray for those we disagree with. To love even when it costs. To seek the good of others, not just the comfort of ourselves. Make us ministers of reconciliation—bridging gaps, healing hearts, standing firm in the Spirit, but always with gentleness and truth.

We ask that You would prosper this nation—not just economically, but in soul, in conscience, in character. Prosper us with wisdom. Prosper us with justice. Prosper us with humility. And may Your name be honored once again in the public square and in every home.

Do it, Lord, not for our glory, but for Yours. That the world may see and know that there is a God in heaven who answers prayer and heals nations.

In Jesus' name, Amen.

Day 2: LET PEACE SPRING FORTH

Thorns and briers will come up on my people's land; yes, on all the houses of joy in the joyous city. For the palace will be forsaken. The populous city will be deserted. The hill and the watchtower will be for dens forever, a delight for wild donkeys, a pasture of flocks; Until the Spirit is poured on us from on high, and the wilderness becomes a fruitful field, and the fruitful field is considered a forest. Then justice will dwell in the wilderness; and righteousness will remain in the fruitful field. The work of righteousness will be peace; and the effect of righteousness, quietness and confidence forever. My people will live in a peaceful habitation, in safe dwellings, and in quiet resting places.
—Isaiah 32:13-18 WEB

O Lord, Righteous King and God of Justice,

We come before You burdened for our land, standing in the gap for a nation that groans beneath the weight of division, strife, and rebellion against Your ways. You have spoken through Your prophet: "Thorns and briers will grow up on the land of My people, yes, on all the houses of joy in the joyous city" (Isaiah 32:13). Lord, this is the condition of our nation—once prosperous and filled with laughter, now fractured and overgrown with the weeds of pride, bitterness, and hatred.

But You are a God of mercy. You promise that when the Spirit is poured out from on high, the wilderness will become a fruitful field, and justice will dwell in the land again. So we cry out: Send Your Spirit, O God! Pour out Your mercy like rain upon our dry and hardened ground. Let righteousness return like the dawn, and may Your justice abide in every city, every court, every home.

We intercede for peace—not a superficial calm, but the true peace that flows from right standing with You. For You declared, *"The work of righteousness will be peace, and the effect of righteousness, quietness and assurance forever"* (Isaiah 32:17). Let that be our portion, O God! Heal the wounds between brothers. Reconcile divided communities. Let mercy triumph over judgment in our hearts and in our systems.

Establish Your people in peaceful dwelling places once more. Let every household be a resting place, every neighborhood a quiet haven, every city a secure dwelling. Sweep away every spirit of confusion, fear, and unrest. Replace them with Your Spirit of wisdom, reconciliation, and holy fear.

We know, Father, that peace and unity cannot be manufactured—they must be Spirit-born. So we wait on You. We stand in the gap until You move. We hold fast to Your Word, believing that what You have spoken, You will fulfill. Restore our nation—not by might, not by power, but by Your Spirit.

In Jesus' name, Amen.

Day 3: UNITY AND PEACE

> I therefore, the prisoner in the Lord, beg you to walk worthily
> of the calling with which you were called, with all lowliness and
> humility, with patience, bearing with one another in love; being
> eager to keep the unity of the Spirit in the bond of peace.
> —Ephesians 4:1-3 WEB

Righteous Father,

We come before You as intercessors standing in the gap for our nation—broken, divided, and in desperate need of Your healing touch. We humble ourselves under Your mighty hand, lifting up the name of Jesus, the Prince of Peace, over this land You have blessed. Your Word in Ephesians calls us to walk worthy of the calling we have received— with all humility, gentleness, and patience, bearing with one another in love. Lord, we confess that as a nation we have failed to do this. Pride has taken root, harshness has taken the place of kindness, and impatience has inflamed our divisions.

Yet in Your mercy, You have not cast us away. So we cry out to You now: Restore us, O God of peace! Make us eager to maintain the unity of the Spirit in the bond of peace. Tear down every wall of hostility—racial, political, generational, and denominational—that separates us. Let the love of Christ compel us toward forgiveness and reconciliation. Where bitterness has taken root, sow seeds of grace. Where anger rules, let Your peace reign.

Father, we ask for a supernatural outpouring of humility and gentleness among Your people. May the Church lead the way in walking with long-suffering and love, not pointing fingers, but extending open arms. Let us be peacemakers, not peacekeepers—bold in truth, yet tender in mercy.

We plead for leaders, communities, and families—bring healing where there is wounding, dialogue where there has been silence, and mutual honor where there has been shame. Unify us under the banner of Christ, and let our shared identity in Him override every lesser allegiance.

Lord, You alone can turn the hearts of a nation. Do it in our day. Let unity and peace rise like a river and sweep across this land, bringing refreshment, revival, and reformation.

In Jesus' name, Amen.

Day 4: SOW PEACE

> But the wisdom that is from above is first pure, then peaceful, gentle, reasonable, full of mercy and good fruits, without partiality, and without hypocrisy. Now the fruit of righteousness is sown in peace by those who make peace.
> —James 3:17-18 WEB

Righteous Father,

We come before You, humbled and broken for the state of our land. Your Word declares that the wisdom from above is first pure, then peaceable, gentle, open to reason, full of mercy and good fruits, impartial and sincere. Lord, we confess that we have strayed far from that wisdom. As a nation, we have sown division instead of peace, pride instead of humility, and self-interest instead of mercy. We have pursued earthly wisdom that is unspiritual and demonic, and it has borne bitter fruit in our streets, our homes, and our institutions.

But You, O God, are the God of peace, and You promise that a harvest of righteousness is sown in peace by those who make peace. So we stand in the gap today, asking You to make us those sowers. Raise up peacemakers in every sphere—leaders who carry the fragrance of Christ, pastors who shepherd with truth and tenderness, citizens who speak with grace and live with conviction.

Lord, uproot the seeds of discord sown by the enemy. Break down the walls of hostility between races, generations, and political parties. Where there is misunderstanding, bring clarity. Where there is offense, bring forgiveness. Where there is injury, bring healing. Let Your Spirit move like wind over dry bones and unite what has been fractured.

We do not ask for a false peace, but for the peace that flows from righteousness—peace that comes when hearts are transformed and truth is embraced. Let mercy triumph over judgment in our land. Let gentleness silence rage. Let purity dissolve corruption.

Father, sow in us the wisdom that is from above. Make the Church a reflection of it first—pure, peaceable, gentle, full of mercy. Let that harvest begin in Your house, and may it spread like wildfire into the nation. We long to see Your Kingdom come, not in part, but in fullness.

In Jesus' name, Amen.

Day 5: MERCY OVER JUDGMENT

For judgment is without mercy to him who has shown no
mercy. Mercy triumphs over judgment.
—James 2:13 WEB

Righteous and Merciful Father,

We come before You, burdened for our nation and broken over the
divisions that grieve Your heart. You have declared in Your Word that
*"judgment without mercy will be shown to anyone who has not been
merciful, but mercy triumphs over judgment."* Lord, we plead for Your
mercy to triumph over the judgment we deserve.

Our land has strayed far from Your ways. We have sown discord, exalted
pride, and turned justice into bitterness. But You, O God, are full of
compassion and long-suffering. You delight in mercy. So we stand in
the gap today, not as accusers, but as intercessors—bearing up our
nation before You, asking for healing, not wrath; reconciliation, not
ruin.

Forgive us, Lord, where we have harbored bitterness, where we have
judged harshly, where we have withheld the very mercy we so
desperately need from You. Forgive the church where we have mirrored
the culture more than Christ. Forgive our leaders where they have ruled
with partiality, and forgive the people where they have refused to listen
to one another in love.

We ask You to release a spirit of mercy across our land—mercy that
humbles hearts, mends broken relationships, and restores unity. Let the
law of love govern our speech and actions. Let compassion triumph over
revenge, and understanding over fear.

Father, raise up peacemakers in every sphere of influence—those who will speak truth in love, those who will build bridges where others build walls. May Your church lead the way in showing mercy, knowing that mercy is the evidence of true faith. Let us not be a people who honor You with lips while our hearts remain far away.

We cry out for reconciliation—across races, denominations, generations, and political divides. Only Your Spirit can heal what man has broken. So, stretch out Your hand and pour out the oil of Your mercy upon every wounded place. Heal our land, not by might, not by power, but by Your Spirit.

Let mercy roll down like waters, and righteousness like an ever-flowing stream.

In Jesus' name, Amen.

Day 6: GIVE US YOUR PEACE

'Yahweh bless you, and keep you. Yahweh make his face to
shine on you, and be gracious to you. Yahweh lift up his face
toward you, and give you peace.'
—Numbers 6:24-26 WEB

O Lord, our Covenant-Keeping God,

We lift our hearts to You in intercession for this nation—broken, weary,
and divided. You are the One who spoke peace over chaos in the
beginning, and You alone can speak peace over our land today.

Lord, we stand in the gap and cry out, "Give us Your peace." Not peace
that the world gives, not the fragile quiet born of avoidance or
compromise, but the shalom that comes from Your throne—a peace
that heals what is shattered, restores what is lost, and binds together
what hatred has torn apart.

Your Word declares, *"The Lord bless you and keep you; the Lord make
His face shine upon you and be gracious to you; the Lord lift up His
countenance upon you and give you peace."* So we ask, Father, bless this
nation—not because we are worthy, but because You are merciful. Keep
us in Your truth, guard us from the lies that divide, and preserve us from
the destruction that comes when sin runs unchecked.

Shine the light of Your face upon our people. Let Your radiant presence
expose the darkness in our hearts and in our systems. Be gracious to us,
Lord—heal generations of wounds, cleanse the stains of injustice, and
raise up voices of reconciliation who speak with Your heart.

Lift up Your countenance upon us, O God. Do not hide Your face from
us in anger, but remember mercy. Look upon our land and breathe life

where there has been death. Bring unity where there is hostility. Silence the enemy's voice that incites fear and rage. Let Your peace fall like rain—saturating our cities, our homes, our leaders, and our churches.

We do not ask for the absence of conflict alone, but for the presence of Your Spirit. May Your peace rule in our hearts and in this nation. Let it crush every dividing wall and draw us to the cross where reconciliation begins.

In Jesus' name, Amen.

Day 7: A COVENANT OF PEACE

> Moreover I will make a covenant of peace with them. It will be an everlasting covenant with them. I will place them, multiply them, and will set my sanctuary among them forever more. My tent also will be with them. I will be their God, and they will be my people. The nations will know that I am Yahweh who sanctifies Israel, when my sanctuary is among them forever more."""
>
> —Ezekiel 37:26-28 WEB

O Lord God of Israel, Keeper of covenant and Lord of peace,

We come before You with hearts bowed low, standing in the gap for our nation. We plead with You, not because of our righteousness, but because of Your great mercy. You have spoken, saying, *"I will make a covenant of peace with them; it shall be an everlasting covenant with them. I will set them in their land and multiply them and set My sanctuary in their midst forevermore."* (Ezekiel 37:26)

Lord, we cry out for that covenant of peace to be made manifest in our day. Let Your everlasting promise stretch over this land like a banner. Where strife has ruled, bring reconciliation. Where division has taken root, plant unity that cannot be shaken. Let Your peace flow like a river through every city, every community, every family—healing the old wounds, tearing down walls of hostility, and reconciling hearts to one another and to You.

You declared, *"My dwelling place shall be with them, and I will be their God, and they shall be My people."* We long for this reality, O God. Dwell among us again. Be enthroned in our midst. Walk in our streets. Rest in our homes. Make Your people holy again—united not by race, region, or politics, but by the blood of Christ and the power of the Spirit.

Let the watching nations know that You, the Lord, have sanctified us, because Your sanctuary is with us forevermore. Make this nation a testimony of Your redeeming power. Let former enemies become brothers, and let justice and mercy kiss at our gates. Raise up peacemakers, truth-bearers, and bridge-builders, and let Your Church lead the way—one voice, one Spirit, one heart.

Lord, make us a people of Your covenant again. Seal this land with peace not forged by men but spoken by You. In every policy, every law, every heart—let the covenant of Your peace reign.

In Jesus' name, Amen.

Day 8: THAT WE MAY BE ONE

Not for these only do I pray, but for those also who will believe
in me through their word, that they may all be one; even as you,
Father, are in me, and I in you, that they also may be one in us;
that the world may believe that you sent me.
—John 17:20-21 WEB

Righteous Father,

We come before You with humble hearts, standing in the gap for our
nation, burdened with division, hatred, and brokenness. Your Son, our
Lord Jesus Christ, prayed, *"I do not pray for these alone, but also for those
who will believe in Me through their word; that they all may be one, as
You, Father, are in Me, and I in You; that they also may be one in Us, that
the world may believe that You sent Me."*

Lord, this is the cry of our hearts today—that we may be one. Not in
name only, not in outward unity, but in the Spirit, in truth, in purpose.
Let the Church in this nation reflect the unity of the Godhead—Father,
Son, and Holy Spirit—so that the watching world will believe. Tear
down the walls of hostility between races, denominations, and political
tribes. Dismantle every root of bitterness, pride, and offense that keeps
us apart.

Father, we ask for the healing oil of Your Spirit to flow across this land.
Heal families torn apart by anger. Heal cities broken by violence. Heal
churches divided by preference and pride. We stand as intercessors,
pleading the prayer of Your Son—make us one, Lord. Make us one in
Your truth, one in Your love, one in Your mission to reach the lost.

May the unity Jesus prayed for be made manifest in our generation. Let
it begin with us. Baptize us in humility. Teach us to prefer one another.

Cause us to see each other not through the lens of flesh, but through the eyes of the Spirit. That we may walk worthy of our calling, bearing with one another in love, endeavoring to keep the unity of the Spirit in the bond of peace.

We renounce the spirit of division and confusion. We silence the voices that stir up strife and discord. And we call forth a new day of reconciliation and kingdom unity—across neighborhoods, pulpits, and governmental halls.

Let the Church rise as one voice, with clean hands and pure hearts, to declare that Jesus is Lord over this nation. And let the love we have for one another be the evidence that You have sent Him.

In Jesus' name, Amen.

Day 9: ONE NATION UNDER GOD

I will make them one nation in the land, on the mountains of
Israel. One king will be king to them all. They will no longer be
two nations. They won't be divided into two kingdoms any
more at all.
—Ezekiel 37:22 WEB

Lord God Almighty,

You are the One who gathers Your people from every corner, from many
tribes and nations, and brings us together as one. Just as You declared
through Your prophet, "I will make them one nation in the land, on the
mountains of Israel; and one king will be king over them all," so now we
stand before You, humbly asking for Your divine intervention in our
nation.

Father, we confess that we have been divided by fear, pride, and
prejudice. We have fractured Your vision of unity and peace. Yet Your
promise remains steadfast: that You will heal our brokenness and bring
reconciliation where there has been strife. We pray now that You would
breathe new life into our hearts and into the soul of this nation.

Bind us together, Lord, with cords that cannot be broken—cords of
righteousness, justice, and love. Raise up leaders who seek Your face
and govern with integrity. Heal the wounds of racial, social, and
political divisions that threaten to tear us apart. Let Your Spirit move
mightily to reconcile differences, restore relationships, and unite us in
one purpose under Your sovereign kingship.

May Your kingdom come and Your will be done across this land, as we
embrace the calling to be one nation under God—reflecting Your glory,

justice, and mercy to the world. Let peace reign in our cities, our homes, and our hearts.

We stand in the gap, Lord, asking for Your holy hand to guide us into a future shaped by Your truth and grace. Fulfill Your covenant promises to this nation, that we might live as a testimony of Your redeeming power.

In Jesus' name, Amen.

Day 10: UNITED IN AN EVERLASTING COVENANT

> "In those days, and in that time," says Yahweh, "the children of Israel will come, they and the children of Judah together; they will go on their way weeping, and will seek Yahweh their God. They will inquire concerning Zion with their faces turned toward it, saying, 'Come, and join yourselves to Yahweh in an everlasting covenant that will not be forgotten.'
> —Jeremiah 50:4-5 WEB

O Lord God of Israel,

You who remember mercy in wrath and covenant in chaos, we come before You with trembling hearts, crying out for our nation. We echo the voice of Your people in days past: "They shall ask the way to Zion with their faces turned toward it, saying, 'Come, let us join ourselves to the Lord in an everlasting covenant that will never be forgotten.'"

Father, our nation has strayed and stumbled, wounded by division and deafened by pride. But You are the God who heals breaches and gathers exiles. Turn our hearts again toward Zion—toward Your dwelling, Your ways, Your name. Stir a holy longing within us for peace not born of compromise, but of covenant. Let the people of this land, from every tribe and tongue, ask again for the ancient paths where the good way lies.

Bind us, O Lord, in a unity forged not by politics or persuasion but by Your Spirit. Join us together in an everlasting covenant sealed by the blood of Your Son—one that will not be broken, one that will not be forgotten. Let reconciliation rise like morning light and let every heart say, "Come, let us return to the Lord."

In Jesus' name, Amen.

Day 11: Come, Let Us Return to the Lord

> "Come! Let's return to Yahweh; for he has torn us to pieces, and he will heal us; he has injured us, and he will bind up our wounds. After two days he will revive us. On the third day he will raise us up, and we will live before him. Let's acknowledge Yahweh. Let's press on to know Yahweh. As surely as the sun rises, Yahweh will appear. He will come to us like the rain, like the spring rain that waters the earth."
> —Hosea 6:1-3 WEB

Lord God, Righteous and Merciful,

We come before You with brokenness in our hearts and hope in our cries, saying together, "Come, let us return to the Lord." For we acknowledge that though You have torn us, You will heal us; though You have struck us down, You will bind us up. We stand in the gap for our nation, pleading not for what we deserve, but for Your mercy and covenant love to rise again upon this land.

Father, we repent for how far we have drifted—from Your Word, from Your ways, and from one another. Where there has been division, bring unity. Where there has been wounding, bring healing. Where pride has hardened hearts, send the rain of Your Spirit to soften us.

You have promised that after two days You will revive us, and on the third day You will raise us up, that we may live before You. So we intercede with faith—revive this generation, O God. Awaken hearts to seek Your face, not just Your hand. Let us know You; let us press on to know You.

As surely as the dawn breaks, so let Your coming renew our land. Let Your righteousness rain down like spring showers upon our weary ground. Restore what was lost, redeem what was broken, and reconcile us to You and to one another.

In Jesus' name, Amen.

Day 12: RETURN AND BE RESTORED

> A voice is heard on the bare heights, the weeping and the petitions of the children of Israel; because they have perverted their way, they have forgotten Yahweh their God. Return, you backsliding children, and I will heal your backsliding. "Behold, we have come to you; for you are Yahweh our God. Truly in vain is help from the hills, the tumult on the mountains. Truly the salvation of Israel is in Yahweh our God.
> —Jeremiah 3:21-23 WEB

Righteous Father,

We hear the voice of our nation weeping upon the heights, a bitter cry from hearts scattered and broken, who have forgotten their resting place in You. Lord, we stand in the gap for this generation—wandering, wounded, deceived—who have placed their trust in hills and idols, in power and pride, but not in the God of their salvation.

We confess on behalf of our people that we have turned from Your voice and followed paths of destruction. Yet Your Word declares: *"Truly in the Lord our God is the salvation of Israel."* We proclaim that truth now over this nation—salvation is not in our systems, alliances, or strength. Salvation is in You alone.

God of mercy, draw hearts to repentance. Let a cry rise from every city, every church, every family: "We have sinned against the Lord!" Let reconciliation flow like a river—between generations, races, and regions. Heal the breaches; restore the ruined places. Awaken the shepherds, stir the watchmen, and break the chains of false peace and superficial unity.

We plead for a holy return to You—our only hope, our true refuge. You are waiting with mercy; let Your kindness lead us to repentance and reconciliation. Let Your Spirit sweep over the land, and let a generation return with weeping and joy.

In Jesus' name, Amen.

Day 13: COME BACK TO MERCY

Seek Yahweh while he may be found. Call on him while he is
near. Let the wicked forsake his way, and the unrighteous man
his thoughts. Let him return to Yahweh, and he will have mercy
on him; and to our God, for he will freely pardon.
—Isaiah 55:6-7 WEB

Righteous and Merciful God,

We seek You while You may be found; we call upon You while You are
near. For our nation, fractured and wandering, we stand in the gap
today. Lord, we cry out on behalf of every heart hardened by division,
every home broken by injustice, every community shaken by strife. You
are near to the brokenhearted, and we believe You still long to heal what
is torn.

Father, You have said, "Let the wicked forsake his way, and the
unrighteous man his thoughts; and let him return to the Lord, and He
will have mercy on him; and to our God, for He will abundantly
pardon." So we intercede, not only for individual repentance but for
national return. Let the proud bow low, the lost come home, and the
weary find rest in Your mercy. Silence every voice of hatred, and awaken
a hunger for righteousness that runs deeper than politics, deeper than
culture—down to the very soul of this land.

Pour out the spirit of reconciliation across generations, races, and
regions. May the blood of Jesus speak louder than the blood of division.
May Your Word be heard in the streets again, calling us not to
condemnation, but to compassion and covenant.

We plead for a revival of mercy, for a revolution of grace. Heal our land, O God—not only by restoring what was, but by reforming us into what You desire.

In Jesus' name, Amen.

Day 14: COME, LET US WALK IN HIS LIGHT

It shall happen in the latter days, that the mountain of Yahweh's house shall be established on the top of the mountains, and shall be raised above the hills; and all nations shall flow to it. Many peoples shall go and say, "Come, let's go up to the mountain of Yahweh, to the house of the God of Jacob; and he will teach us of his ways, and we will walk in his paths." For out of Zion the law shall go out, and Yahweh's word from Jerusalem. He will judge between the nations, and will decide concerning many peoples; and they shall beat their swords into plowshares, and their spears into pruning hooks. Nation shall not lift up sword against nation, neither shall they learn war any more. House of Jacob, come, and let's walk in the light of Yahweh.

—Isaiah 2:2-5 WEB

Lord God Almighty,

You are the Judge of the nations and the Shepherd of peoples. In the last days, Your mountain shall be exalted above all, and all nations shall stream to it. So we come before You, standing in the gap for our nation, crying out for the fulfillment of Your Word—that we would turn from war to peace, from pride to humility, from division to divine unity.

Father, we ask that You draw the hearts of our people to Your holy hill, that we may be taught Your ways and walk in Your paths. Let every hardened heart be softened by the invitation of Your Spirit. Let swords be beaten into plowshares—strife exchanged for service, hatred replaced with healing. We plead for reconciliation to spring forth like dawn, and for unity to rise like the noonday sun over a land long shadowed by bitterness and brokenness.

Forgive us for walking in darkness, for exalting our own ways above Yours. We confess that peace cannot come by the hands of men alone—it must come by the light of Your truth. So Lord, shine Your light upon this nation. Call us to walk in it. May families, leaders, and communities align with Your justice, live in Your peace, and reflect the radiance of Your Kingdom.

We believe Your Word will not return void. You will restore. You will reconcile. You will reform.

In Jesus' name, Amen.

SECTION 2:

MORALITY, TRUTH & RIGHTEOUS LEADERSHIP

A nation cannot stand without truth. When morality collapses and lies go unchallenged, darkness spreads, justice falters, and the people suffer. Scripture warns that when *"truth is fallen in the streets"* (Isaiah 59:14), righteousness cannot enter—and without righteousness, a nation loses its way. But God is still raising up a remnant who will cry out for truth to rise again, for hearts to return to holiness, and for leaders who fear the Lord more than public opinion.

This section calls us to bold intercession for the moral and spiritual fabric of our land. Here we ask God to expose corruption, restore truth in our pulpits and public offices, and raise up leaders marked by integrity, humility, and courage. We confess the sins of deception, pride, and compromise, and we stand in the gap for a generation that's forgotten the difference between good and evil. As you pray through these themes, let your voice be one that calls a nation back to righteousness—because when truth leads, freedom follows, and when righteousness rules, the people rejoice.

Day 15: RIGHTEOUS FOUNDATIONS

If the foundations are destroyed, what can the righteous do?
—Psalms 11:3 WEB

Righteous Father,

You are the Judge of all the earth, and Your throne is established in righteousness and justice. Your eyes see, Your eyelids test the sons of men. Today we come before You, burdened for our nation. You have said in Your Word, "If the foundations are destroyed, what can the righteous do?" (Psalm 11:3). Lord, we stand in the gap—crying out for the restoration of righteous foundations in our land.

Forgive us, O God, for turning from Your truth and calling evil good and good evil. We repent on behalf of our nation for forsaking Your Word, for compromising integrity in leadership, for silencing Your voice in our laws and our culture. We plead for mercy where there has been corruption, deception, and injustice.

Raise up leaders who fear You—men and women whose hearts are guided by truth, whose judgments are shaped by righteousness, and whose decisions reflect Your justice. Expose the works of darkness and bring them to light. Let truth prevail in every institution—government, media, education, business, and the church.

Establish once again the ancient paths. Rebuild the moral walls. Restore Your Word as the plumb line for truth in our land. Let Your righteousness rain down like a river and justice like an ever-flowing stream.

We declare that You, Lord, are still on the throne. Though the foundations may be shaken, You remain unshakable. We take refuge in

You, and we ask You to make us bold, faithful intercessors until Your will is done on earth as it is in heaven.

In Jesus' name, Amen.

Day 16: TRUTH IN THE HALLS OF POWER

You will know the truth, and the truth will make you free."
—John 8:32 WEB

Righteous Father, the God of all truth,

We come before You with brokenness and boldness, pleading for our nation. You have said, "Then you will know the truth, and the truth will set you free" (John 8:32). We confess, Lord, that deception has crept into the halls of power—into legislation, leadership, and judgment. Truth has stumbled in the public square, and righteousness stands at a distance. But You, O Lord, are the God who cannot lie, and Your Word is forever settled in heaven.

We ask You to pierce through every veil of darkness with the blazing light of Your truth. Expose corruption, uproot dishonesty, and silence every lying tongue that exalts itself against the knowledge of God. Raise up leaders who fear You—who do not twist justice, who do not trade truth for power, who will walk in integrity and lead with wisdom from above. Let righteousness flow like a river, and truth like an unending stream through every branch of government, media, and education.

Let Your people be bold in truth and tender in mercy, refusing to compromise. Let Your Word be our standard again. And may the truth that is Jesus Christ set this nation free—spiritually, morally, and politically.

In Jesus' name, Amen.

Day 17: Restore Truth To Its Place

> The army was given over to it together with the continual burnt offering through disobedience. It cast down truth to the ground, and it did its pleasure and prospered.
> —Daniel 8:12 WEB

O Sovereign Lord, Righteous and Just,

We come before You burdened for a nation that has cast truth to the ground. As in the days of Daniel, deception has been exalted, and truth has been trampled beneath pride, compromise, and corruption. But You, O God, are the God of all truth, and Your Word stands forever. You judge with righteousness, and You see every hidden lie and every public distortion.

Father, we stand in the gap for our nation—pleading with You to restore truth to its rightful place. Tear down every system, policy, and platform that promotes falsehood. Expose every lie and uproot every deceitful agenda. Let truth no longer be silenced, twisted, or weaponized. As Daniel saw, rebellion flourished when truth was overthrown—but we ask for a reversal. We ask for truth to rise and rebellion to fall.

Raise up leaders who love the truth, speak the truth, and live by Your truth. Let righteousness and justice once again be the foundation of our government, and may integrity mark those who lead. Teach us, Your people, to discern truth from error and to stand boldly for what is right—even when it costs us.

Lord, shine Your light in the darkness. Let truth triumph over propaganda, purity over perversion, and wisdom over wickedness. We repent for the ways we have allowed truth to be compromised, and we ask You to cleanse our hearts, our pulpits, our courts, and our classrooms.

Restore truth, Lord—not just as a principle, but as the Person of Christ reigning in every sphere of influence in our land.

In Jesus' name, Amen.

Day 18: Truth Stumbles in the Streets

> Justice is turned away backward, and righteousness stands far away; for truth has fallen in the street, and uprightness can't enter. Yes, truth is lacking; and he who departs from evil makes himself a prey. Yahweh saw it, and it displeased him that there was no justice. He saw that there was no man, and wondered that there was no intercessor. Therefore his own arm brought salvation to him; and his righteousness sustained him.
> —Isaiah 59:14-16 WEB

Righteous Father,

We come before You in brokenness, recognizing the condition of our land. Justice has turned back. Righteousness stands far off. Truth has stumbled in the streets, and uprightness cannot enter. You see it all, O Lord, and it grieves Your heart. You looked for justice—but found none; for a man to intercede—but were astonished that there was no one.

Today, we step into that gap.

Raise up intercessors who will not be silent, who will weep between the porch and the altar, crying out for righteousness to return to our government, our pulpits, our communities, and our homes. Let truth be exalted again in our courts, in our media, in our classrooms, and in every sphere where deception has reigned.

We repent for the compromise, for the silence in the face of wickedness, and for leaders who have called evil good and good evil. We cry out for a holy reformation—a turning back to Your Word, Your ways, and Your standard of truth.

Let Your arm not only bring salvation, but also raise up righteous leaders—bold in truth, humble in heart, unshakable in integrity. Let

Your justice roll down like waters, and Your righteousness like an ever-flowing stream.

In Jesus' name, Amen.

Day 19: FLATTERING LIPS AND A DOUBLE HEART

For the Chief Musician; upon an eight-stringed lyre. A Psalm of David. Help, Yahweh; for the godly man ceases. For the faithful fail from among the children of men. Everyone lies to his neighbor. They speak with flattering lips, and with a double heart. May Yahweh cut off all flattering lips, and the tongue that boasts, who have said, "With our tongue we will prevail. Our lips are our own. Who is lord over us?" "Because of the oppression of the weak and because of the groaning of the needy, I will now arise," says Yahweh; "I will set him in safety from those who malign him."
—Psalms 12:1-5 WEB

Righteous Father,

We cry out to You today with the heart of the psalmist, for the godly are vanishing and the faithful are few among the children of men. Truth has stumbled in the streets, and deception flows freely from lips that flatter and hearts that deceive. Lord, we see the fruit of prideful tongues—those who say, "With our tongue we will prevail; our lips are our own—who is lord over us?" But You, O Lord, are not mocked. You see. You hear. You are righteous altogether.

We stand in the gap on behalf of our nation, pleading for Your mercy. Where truth has been traded for lies, restore righteousness. Where leaders speak with double hearts, raise up those who fear You and walk in integrity. Let the fire of Your Word refine our speech and purify our hearts. Silence the boasting tongue and expose every hidden motive. Let leaders who lead in justice and truth arise—those whose yes is yes and no is no, whose words bring healing and not harm.

For the oppression of the poor, for the sighing of the needy, You have promised to arise. Arise, O Lord. Defend the weak. Break the power of deceptive speech. Make Your words—pure as silver, refined in a furnace—fill the mouths of those You raise up in this hour. Let truth spring from the ground, and righteousness look down from heaven.

In Jesus' name, Amen.

Day 20: They Swear Falsely

"Run back and forth through the streets of Jerusalem, and see now, and know, and seek in its wide places, if you can find a man, if there is anyone who does justly, who seeks truth, then I will pardon her. Though they say, 'As Yahweh lives,' surely they swear falsely."
—Jeremiah 5:1-2 WEB

Righteous Judge of all the earth,

You who search the hearts of men and test the thoughts of every soul—look upon our land with mercy. You commanded, "Go up and down the streets of Jerusalem... look for one who deals honestly and seeks the truth." Yet Lord, even as Your eyes run to and fro throughout the earth, You find so few who walk uprightly. Our nation has turned truth into a lie, and righteousness into a byword. Many speak Your name, but not in truth or justice—they swear falsely, and yet claim to know You.

We stand in the gap today, burdened with the weight of national deception. We cry out for the leaders, the lawmakers, the judges, and those in high places who have exchanged integrity for gain and justice for corruption. Forgive us, O God, for calling evil good and good evil. Tear down the altars built to self-interest, and raise up shepherds who fear Your name, who tremble at Your Word, and who lead with righteousness and truth.

Remember Your covenant, Lord. Do not forsake us, though we have sinned greatly. Let there arise a generation who will not swear falsely, but will walk in truth, love mercy, and do justice. Heal our hearts so that truth may dwell in our streets again.

In Jesus' name, Amen.

Day 21: THERE IS NO TRUTH IN THE LAND

Hear Yahweh's word, you children of Israel; for Yahweh has a charge against the inhabitants of the land: "Indeed there is no truth, nor goodness, nor knowledge of God in the land. There is cursing, lying, murder, stealing, and committing adultery; they break boundaries, and bloodshed causes bloodshed. Therefore the land will mourn, and everyone who dwells therein will waste away. all living things in her, even the animals of the field and the birds of the sky; yes, the fish of the sea also die.

—Hosea 4:1-3 WEB

Lord God Almighty,

Your Word declares that there is no truth, no mercy, no knowledge of You in the land. The earth mourns, the heavens grow dark, and even the animals suffer because of the sin and rebellion that flood this nation. Yet, You are the God who hears the cries of Your people and who calls us to stand in the gap, to intercede and plead for Your mercy.

Father, we come before You with broken hearts, confessing the decay of truth and righteousness that has taken hold in our leaders and among our people. Our land is fractured by lies, injustice, and moral blindness. We recognize that without Your truth ruling in the hearts of those in authority and in the streets of our nation, destruction is inevitable.

But You are a God of restoration and healing. We ask You now to raise up righteous leaders who fear You, who seek Your wisdom and justice above all else. Let them be lights in the darkness, bearers of Your truth, and stewards of Your righteousness. Restore the knowledge of You across every community and every heart.

Lord, as Your prophets of old stood in the gap, so we stand today, pleading for Your mercy to cover this land. Do not let Your anger consume us; turn us back to Yourself. Let Your healing waters flow and wash away the corruption, deceit, and wickedness that have taken root. Revive our souls with Your faithfulness and love.

We declare Your sovereignty over this nation and ask that Your kingdom come and Your will be done, on earth as it is in heaven. Let truth be restored, let mercy triumph, and let righteousness reign.

In Jesus' name, Amen.

Day 22: The Godly Man Has Perished

The godly man has perished out of the earth, and there is no one upright among men. They all lie in wait for blood; every man hunts his brother with a net. Their hands are on that which is evil to do it diligently. The ruler and judge ask for a bribe; and the powerful man dictates the evil desire of his soul. Thus they conspire together. The best of them is like a brier. The most upright is worse than a thorn hedge. The day of your watchmen, even your visitation, has come; now is the time of their confusion.

—Micah 7:2-4 WEB

Lord God Almighty,

We come before You with heavy hearts, burdened by the truth that the godly man has perished, and faithful men are nowhere to be found in our land. Our eyes search desperately for leaders who walk in Your righteousness and integrity, yet so often we see only those who love evil and chase after gain. We mourn the brokenness and the decay of morality that threatens to consume this nation.

Father, in Your mercy, hear the cries of Your people who stand in the gap. Raise up men and women after Your own heart—those who will not only lead with truth but embody it in every action, every decision, every moment. Let righteousness be the foundation of their leadership, and justice the standard by which they govern.

We ask, Lord, that You would heal the wounds caused by deceit, betrayal, and corruption. Restore honor where it has been lost and bring revival to our communities through godly example. Let Your Spirit move mightily to expose the darkness and illuminate the path of truth.

Strengthen us, Your servants, to intercede boldly, to stand unwaveringly in the breach, and to pray without ceasing for the restoration of holiness and uprightness in every sphere of influence. May our nation be a reflection of Your kingdom, a beacon of hope grounded in Your unchanging truth.

Father, bring forth leaders who fear You, who hate covetousness, and who will not be swayed by bribes or lies. Let righteousness flow like a mighty river, cleansing and transforming every heart and every institution.

We trust Your sovereign hand to turn the hearts of rulers and restore justice in the land. May Your kingdom come, and Your will be done on earth as it is in heaven.

In Jesus' name, Amen.

Day 23: CLEANSE OUR COURTS

> You shall not pervert justice. You shall not show partiality. You shall not take a bribe, for a bribe blinds the eyes of the wise, and perverts the words of the righteous. You shall follow that which is altogether just, that you may live, and inherit the land which Yahweh your God gives you.
> —Deuteronomy 16:19-20 WEB

Lord God Almighty,

You who command justice and call us to uphold righteousness without partiality or bribery, we come before You now, standing in the gap for our nation. Your Word says, "You shall not pervert justice; you shall not show partiality, and you shall not accept a bribe, for a bribe blinds the eyes of the wise and twists the words of the righteous." Father, we confess the times when justice has been compromised, when truth has been bent, and when righteousness has been overshadowed by corruption in our courts and leadership.

Cleanse our courts, O Lord. Purify the hearts and minds of judges, magistrates, and all who serve in positions of authority. Remove the scales of favoritism and selfish gain that cloud judgment. Empower them to act justly, love mercy, and walk humbly before You, so that justice may flow like a mighty river throughout our land.

May Your righteousness be established as the foundation of every decision, and may truth prevail in every courtroom and council. Raise up leaders who fear You, who hate unjust gain, and who govern with integrity. Let Your justice roll down like waters and Your righteousness like an ever-flowing stream.

We stand in the gap, interceding not by our own strength, but by Your Spirit working in us, asking that Your plans for reconciliation, righteousness, and reformation be fulfilled in this nation. Let us be a people who seek justice, love mercy, and walk in Your truth, for only then can our land be healed and restored.

In Jesus' name, Amen.

Day 24: Truth In Our Pulpits

Preach the word; be urgent in season and out of season;
reprove, rebuke, and exhort, with all patience and teaching. For
the time will come when they will not listen to the sound
doctrine, but, having itching ears, will heap up for themselves
teachers after their own lusts; and will turn away their ears from
the truth, and turn away to fables.
—2 Timothy 4:2-4 WEB

Lord God Almighty,

You who know the hearts of all men and the deep struggles of our times,
we come before You as humble intercessors, standing in the gap for our
nation. You have called us to proclaim Your Word boldly, to preach the
truth in season and out of season, to reprove, rebuke, and exhort with
all patience and careful instruction. Father, we confess that many voices
in our land have drifted away from Your truth, turning to myths and
flattering speech, neglecting the power of Your living Word. We cry out
to You now—revive in our pulpits the courage to declare Your
unchanging truth without compromise. Raise up shepherds who will
not shrink from confrontation but will faithfully lead with integrity,
wisdom, and righteousness.

We ask for Your Spirit to ignite a holy fire within those who stand before
Your people, that they might speak life and conviction, that hearts
would be pierced and minds awakened. Remove the veil of deception
and fear that keeps truth from being spoken and received. Father, let
Your Word be a lamp to the feet of leaders and citizens alike, guiding
them in paths of righteousness for Your name's sake.

We pray for a sweeping awakening of morality grounded in Your eternal standards, a turning back to the foundation of Your righteousness and justice. Let truth once more define our conversations, our laws, and our leaders' decisions. Empower Your servants to call out sin boldly and to point all to the hope found only in Christ Jesus.

May Your kingdom come and Your will be done in our nation as in heaven. We stand firm on Your promises, trusting that You hear the cries of Your people and will move mightily to restore what has been broken.

In Jesus' name, Amen.

Day 25: Return to Righteousness

"Thus has Yahweh of Armies spoken, saying, 'Execute true judgment, and show kindness and compassion every man to his brother. Don't oppress the widow, nor the fatherless, the foreigner, nor the poor; and let none of you devise evil against his brother in your heart.' But they refused to listen, and turned their backs, and stopped their ears, that they might not hear. Yes, they made their hearts as hard as flint, lest they might hear the law, and the words which Yahweh of Armies had sent by his Spirit by the former prophets. Therefore great wrath came from Yahweh of Armies. It has come to pass that, as he called, and they refused to listen, so they will call, and I will not listen," said Yahweh of Armies; "but I will scatter them with a whirlwind among all the nations which they have not known. Thus the land was desolate after them, so that no man passed through nor returned: for they made the pleasant land desolate."
—Zechariah 7:9-14 WEB

Righteous Judge and Merciful Father,

You have spoken through the prophets, declaring, *"Execute true justice, show mercy and compassion everyone to his brother."* But we confess, Lord, as a nation we have turned away. We have hardened our hearts like flint and refused to hear Your law or heed the cries of the oppressed. Our leaders have often loved power more than justice, and our people have chosen comfort over truth. Yet You are still calling.

We stand in the gap, Lord, pleading for mercy over judgment. Tear down every lie that exalts itself against the knowledge of You. Raise up leaders who fear You and love righteousness—who will not turn their backs on the widow, the orphan, or the stranger. Where stubbornness has brought desolation, we cry out for a spirit of repentance. Let hearts once scattered by rebellion be gathered again in humility.

Let Your justice flow like a river and righteousness like a never-failing stream. Soften hearts across this land—especially among those in authority. Replace pride with compassion, corruption with integrity, deception with truth. And let the fear of the Lord once again be the beginning of wisdom in our courts, our schools, our homes, and our government.

In Jesus' name, Amen.

Day 26: SOW IN RIGHTEOUSNESS, REAP IN MERCY

> Sow to yourselves in righteousness, reap according to kindness. Break up your fallow ground; for it is time to seek Yahweh, until he comes and rains righteousness on you. You have plowed wickedness. You have reaped iniquity. You have eaten the fruit of lies, for you trusted in your way, in the multitude of your mighty men.
> —Hosea 10:12-13 WEB

Righteous Father, we come before You on behalf of this nation—broken in many ways, yet beloved by You. You have said in Your Word, "Sow to yourselves in righteousness, reap in mercy; break up your fallow ground: for it is time to seek the Lord, till He come and rain righteousness upon you." And so, we stand in the gap now, lifting our voices and hearts before Your throne, pleading for divine mercy and holy rain.

Lord, we confess that we have too often plowed in wickedness and reaped iniquity. We have trusted in our own way, in our own strength, and in the multitude of our might. But today, we cry out for the plow of Your Spirit to break the hardness in our hearts and in the systems of this land. Let every fallow place—every unyielding, resistant soul—be softened by the water of repentance.

Sow into this nation seeds of righteousness, Lord. Raise up those who will plant truth, justice, and humility in the soil of Your Word. Let mercy spring up like a harvest too great to count. Let Your righteousness rain down upon every region—flooding our cities, saturating our schools, soaking our families, and reviving our government with holy fear.

May this be the hour we truly seek You—not with lip service, but with torn hearts and trembling spirits. May our seeking not cease until You come with power, until mercy prevails over judgment, and until the destiny You ordained for this nation is fully awakened.

In Jesus' name, Amen.

Day 27: DELIVER US FROM LYING LIPS

Deliver my soul, Yahweh, from lying lips, from a deceitful tongue. What will be given to you, and what will be done more to you, you deceitful tongue? Sharp arrows of the mighty, with coals of juniper.
—Psalms 120:2-4 WEB

Deliver us, O Lord, from lying lips and from a deceitful tongue. We come before You as intercessors, broken by the dishonesty that has corrupted our land—words twisted for power, truth suppressed for gain. You are the God of truth, and Your Word is pure. We cry out for a righteous standard to be raised once again across our nation.

Let the arrows of deception be shattered by the power of Your Word. Let every tongue that speaks lies for personal ambition or political control be silenced by Your justice. We stand in the gap, pleading for those blinded by falsehoods, asking You to open their eyes and soften their hearts.

Expose every hidden agenda that wars against truth. Cleanse the public square of flattery and manipulation. Let leaders rise who walk in integrity, whose speech is seasoned with wisdom and whose counsel comes from the fear of the Lord. Replace manipulation with honesty, corruption with purity, and confusion with clarity.

Let the coals of Heaven touch the lips of our leaders and our people, burning away deceit and igniting a hunger for righteousness. Have mercy on us, and restore truth to the heart of this nation.

In Jesus' name, Amen.

Day 28: GOD-FEARING LEADERSHIP

> Moreover you shall provide out of all the people able men which fear God: men of truth, hating unjust gain; and place such over them, to be rulers of thousands, rulers of hundreds, rulers of fifties, and rulers of tens. Let them judge the people at all times. It shall be that every great matter they shall bring to you, but every small matter they shall judge themselves. So shall it be easier for you, and they shall share the load with you.
> —Exodus 18:21-22 WEB

Righteous and Sovereign Lord,

You are the God who governs with justice and truth. From everlasting to everlasting, Your throne is established in righteousness. We come before You today with hearts burdened for our nation, crying out for leaders who fear You—men and women of integrity, wisdom, and truth.

Your Word in Exodus 18:21-22 gives us the standard: to appoint capable men who fear God, love truth, and hate dishonest gain—leaders who will carry the weight of governance with honor and humility. Lord, we confess that we have strayed from this standard. We have elevated charisma over character, and strategy over righteousness. Forgive us, Lord, for choosing leaders who serve themselves rather than serve You and Your purposes.

Raise up, O God, a generation of leaders who tremble at Your Word. Let their hearts be anchored in truth, not swayed by political gain or public applause. Give us leaders who walk in the fear of the Lord and who uphold justice for the oppressed, the vulnerable, and the voiceless.

We ask for a cleansing in every level of leadership—local, state, and national. Root out corruption and deception. Replace compromise with courage. May Your Spirit rest upon those You appoint, giving them discernment, strength, and the wisdom of Jethro's counsel.

Let righteousness exalt this nation again. May godly leadership be a beacon of Your Kingdom order, and may Your people recognize and support those whom You have truly called.

We stand in the gap, pleading for leaders who will shepherd this nation in the fear of God and in the path of truth. Let Your justice roll down like waters, and Your righteousness like an ever-flowing stream.

In Jesus' name, Amen.

Day 29: Strengthen the Upright

For the scepter of wickedness won't remain over the allotment of the righteous; so that the righteous won't use their hands to do evil. Do good, Yahweh, to those who are good, to those who are upright in their hearts. But as for those who turn away to their crooked ways, Yahweh will lead them away with the workers of iniquity. Peace be on Israel.
—Psalms 125:3-5 WEB

Righteous and Sovereign God,

You are the sure foundation of those who trust in You—those who are like Mount Zion, unshaken and enduring forever. We come before You on behalf of this nation, pleading for Your divine protection over the upright in heart. Your Word declares that the scepter of wickedness shall not rest upon the land allotted to the righteous, lest they stretch out their hands to do wrong. So, Father, we ask You now—uphold and strengthen those who walk in integrity and truth. Strengthen their resolve. Let not the pressures of compromise or corruption wear them down.

Raise up righteous leaders, Lord—leaders whose hearts are tethered to Your Word and whose decisions are shaped by truth, not popular opinion. Let the fear of the Lord govern their judgments. Guard them from being swayed by the influence of the wicked. Surround them with wise counsel and shield them from every scheme that would seek to silence or remove them.

We pray for a shaking that removes every pretense and deception in leadership. Separate the just from the unjust. Let those who do evil be led away in their own crookedness, even as You bless and preserve the upright in their way.

Do good, O Lord, to those who are good and to those who are upright in their hearts. May their voices grow louder, their influence grow stronger, and their light shine brighter in these dark times. Establish their feet in righteousness and let their example awaken a generation to stand boldly for truth.

In Jesus' name, Amen.

SECTION 3:

NATIONAL RESTORATION & REFORMATION

God is not finished with this nation. Even in times of great shaking, He is still the Restorer of ruins and the Rebuilder of broken foundations. Throughout Scripture, whenever His people humbled themselves, turned from sin, and returned to Him, God responded—not with wrath, but with mercy. He revived dry bones. He rebuilt devastated cities. He brought beauty from ashes and joy from mourning. That same power is available today.

In this final section, we cry out for deep and lasting restoration—not just of what's been lost, but of what's been divinely purposed. These prayers are bold and prophetic, asking God to redeem the years stolen by sin and compromise, to bring reformation to our systems and institutions, and to pour out His Spirit in a fresh, undeniable way. We believe for revival that begins in hearts but sweeps across cities, campuses, and capitals. As you pray, ask God to begin that restoration in you—and let your voice join the chorus of intercessors calling forth a new day for the nation. This is not just about healing the past—it's about preparing the way for God's future.

Day 30: RESTORE OUR LOST YEARS

> I will restore to you the years that the swarming locust has
> eaten, the great locust, the grasshopper, and the caterpillar, my
> great army, which I sent among you. You will have plenty to eat,
> and be satisfied, and will praise the name of Yahweh, your God,
> who has dealt wondrously with you; and my people will never
> again be disappointed. You will know that I am among Israel,
> and that I am Yahweh, your God, and there is no one else; and
> my people will never again be disappointed.
> —Joel 2:25-27 WEB

O Lord, our Restorer and Redeemer,

We come before You with broken hearts and humbled spirits, crying out
for our land. You have said, "I will restore to you the years that the
swarming locust has eaten." God of mercy, we bring before You the
wasted years of division, injustice, compromise, and rebellion against
Your truth. We repent for the times our nation has turned away from
You, and we ask now for Your mercy to overshadow our failures.

Where the enemy devoured generations through violence, hatred, and
spiritual apathy—restore. Where hope was stolen by cycles of poverty,
addiction, and despair—restore. Where Your name was dishonored
and Your Word rejected—restore. Pour out healing like rain upon the
dry places of our history. Revive the hearts of leaders, pastors, parents,
and children. Rebuild what was torn down by sin, and reform the
structures that do not reflect Your righteousness.

You promised that we shall eat in plenty and be satisfied, and that Your
people will never be put to shame. Let it be so again in this land. May
our nation know that You are in our midst and that You alone are God.

Raise up a generation that walks in truth, justice, and the fear of the Lord.

We stand in the gap, contending for restoration—not just of fortunes, but of faith, honor, and destiny. Fulfill Your word, O Lord, and glorify Your name in this nation once more.

In Jesus' name, Amen.

Day 31: RESTORE OUR FORTUNES AGAIN

A Song of Ascents. When Yahweh brought back those who returned to Zion, we were like those who dream. Then our mouth was filled with laughter, and our tongue with singing. Then they said among the nations, "Yahweh has done great things for them." Yahweh has done great things for us, and we are glad. Restore our fortunes again, Yahweh, like the streams in the Negev.
—Psalms 126:1-4 WEB

Lord God of mercy and restoration,

When You restored the fortunes of Zion, it was like a dream—our mouths were filled with laughter and our tongues with songs of joy. We remember, O God, how the nations declared, "The Lord has done great things for them." And truly, You have done great things for us—we rejoice in Your faithfulness.

Yet now, Lord, we come with tears, standing in the gap for our nation, crying out for Your healing and renewal. We are a people in need of revival. We confess the broken places—our injustice, our division, our pride—and we turn our hearts to You. Just as streams refresh the dry desert, we ask You to pour out Your Spirit on this land again.

Restore our fortunes, Lord—not merely material, but the fortune of righteousness, the treasure of truth, the wealth of godly leadership and holy fear. Let this generation witness Your hand move in undeniable ways. Let old wounds be healed, let corrupt systems be reformed, and let destinies long delayed be fulfilled by Your mighty power.

We stand as intercessors on behalf of this nation—not to accuse, but to appeal to Your covenant love. Do it again, Lord. Restore us again.

In Jesus' name, Amen.

Day 32: STRENGTHEN US AGAIN

"I will strengthen the house of Judah, and I will save the house of Joseph, and I will bring them back; for I have mercy on them; and they will be as though I had not cast them off: for I am Yahweh their God, and I will hear them. Ephraim will be like a mighty man, and their heart will rejoice as through wine; yes, their children will see it, and rejoice. Their heart will be glad in Yahweh. I will signal for them, and gather them; for I have redeemed them; and they will increase as they have increased. I will sow them among the peoples; and they will remember me in far countries; and they will live with their children, and will return.
—Zechariah 10:6-9 WEB

Lord God of Heaven's Armies,

You who remember mercy and speak promises over Your people— We come as intercessors, standing in the gap for our nation. You declared in Zechariah that You would strengthen the house of Judah and save the house of Joseph. So we cry out: strengthen us again, O God. Revive what has been weakened by sin, division, and despair.

You said, *"I will restore them because I have compassion on them"*—and we cling to that word. Restore what has been scattered. Heal what has been broken. You are the God who does not abandon the works of Your hands. Raise up sons and daughters who remember You—who walk in Your ways with courage and faith.

Cause us to be like mighty warriors, whose hearts are anchored in truth and justice. May we, as a people, return to You—not in formality, but in Spirit and truth. Let joy return to our land, and the sound of repentance lead to national reformation.

Plant us in Your purposes. Whistle for Your scattered ones, and gather us by Your hand. We believe that though we were far, You are bringing us near again—to inherit destiny, to reflect Your glory, to become a testimony of Your covenant love.

In Jesus' name, Amen.

Day 33: GREATER GLORY

This is the word that I covenanted with you when you came out of Egypt, and my Spirit lived among you. 'Don't be afraid.' For this is what Yahweh of Armies says: 'Yet once, it is a little while, and I will shake the heavens, the earth, the sea, and the dry land; and I will shake all nations. The precious things of all nations will come, and I will fill this house with glory, says Yahweh of Armies. The silver is mine, and the gold is mine,' says Yahweh of Armies. 'The latter glory of this house will be greater than the former,' says Yahweh of Armies; 'and in this place I will give peace,' says Yahweh of Armies."
—Haggai 2:5-9 WEB

Lord God Almighty,

You who spoke through Your prophet Haggai, declaring, "I am with you," we come before You now, standing in the gap for our nation. You promised that the glory of this latter house would be greater than the former—Father, we long to see that greater glory rise upon our land once more. Let Your Spirit move mightily to restore what has been broken, to heal what has been wounded, and to renew what has been lost.

We ask for Your divine presence to overshadow every corner of this nation, fulfilling Your promise that You will shake the heavens and the earth, the sea and the dry land, so that the desire of all nations will come. May Your Kingdom come and Your will be done on this soil, Lord, shaping our destiny according to Your perfect plan. Empower us to walk in righteousness and holiness, and grant us the courage to seek Your face with humble hearts.

Lord, as we stand in the gap, we intercede for reconciliation among Your people, for justice to reign, and for reformation to take root in every sphere of influence. May Your glory fill this land in a way that surpasses all past seasons. Let the foundation of this nation be built on Your truth and grace, so that generations to come will know Your name and walk in Your ways.

We trust Your promise, Lord, that You are with us—strengthen us in this hour to persevere until Your glory is fully revealed. We ask all this in the mighty and matchless name of Jesus.

In Jesus' name, Amen.

Day 34: FROM TODAY, BLESS US

'Consider, please, from this day and backward, from the twenty-fourth day of the ninth month, since the day that the foundation of Yahweh's temple was laid, consider it. Is the seed yet in the barn? Yes, the vine, the fig tree, the pomegranate, and the olive tree haven't produced. From today I will bless you.'"
—Haggai 2:18-19 WEB

Lord God Almighty,

You who spoke through Your prophet Haggai, calling Your people to consider their ways and promising blessing from this day forward—hear our cry as we stand in the gap for our nation. We acknowledge the times of delay, the seasons of hardship, and the valleys of loss that have tested us. Yet, Your Word gives hope: from this day, You will bless us. You will bless the seed we sow and the work of our hands.

Father, we repent for the ways we have turned from Your statutes and invite Your cleansing fire to purify our hearts and our land. Restore us, O Lord, and bring reformation that aligns our nation with Your righteousness and justice. Let Your glory fill our cities, our leaders, and every family. May Your presence rise as a mighty wave of restoration that cannot be contained.

We claim Your promise that from this day, You will bless us. Bless the seeds of repentance sown in humility. Bless the efforts of those who seek justice and mercy. Bless the prayers lifted up by those who intercede with faith. Let this be a turning point where Your destiny for this nation unfolds according to Your perfect will.

Give us strength, God, to stand unwavering as intercessors—standing in the gap, not moving aside until Your Kingdom comes and Your will is done on earth as it is in heaven. Let Your peace, power, and presence be our portion now and forevermore.

In Jesus' name, Amen.

Day 35: Turn Our Mourning Into Joy

Behold, I will bring them from the north country, and gather them from the uttermost parts of the earth, along with the blind and the lame, the woman with child and her who travails with child together. They will return as a great company. They will come with weeping. I will lead them with petitions. I will cause them to walk by rivers of waters, in a straight way in which they won't stumble; for I am a father to Israel. Ephraim is my firstborn. "Hear Yahweh's word, you nations, and declare it in the distant islands. Say, 'He who scattered Israel will gather him, and keep him, as a shepherd does his flock.' For Yahweh has ransomed Jacob, and redeemed him from the hand of him who was stronger than he. They will come and sing in the height of Zion, and will flow to the goodness of Yahweh, to the grain, to the new wine, to the oil, and to the young of the flock and of the herd. Their soul will be as a watered garden. They will not sorrow any more at all. Then the virgin will rejoice in the dance; the young men and the old together; for I will turn their mourning into joy, and will comfort them, and make them rejoice from their sorrow. I will satiate the soul of the priests with fatness, and my people will be satisfied with my goodness," says Yahweh.
—Jeremiah 31:8-14 WEB

Lord God Almighty, Creator of heaven and earth, You who gather Your people from the ends of the earth and carry them tenderly as a shepherd carries the lambs—hear our cry today. We stand in the gap for this nation, for Your promises and plans to be fulfilled, longing for Your restoration to sweep over our land.

Father, You have spoken through Your prophet Jeremiah that though we may mourn now, Your steadfast love will turn our sorrow into joy. We lift up our mourning hearts before You, knowing that You are the God who heals the brokenhearted and binds up their wounds. In the midst of loss and division, breathe new life into our communities. Restore what has been broken, reconcile what has been torn apart, and bring forth righteousness that establishes lasting peace.

We ask, Lord, that Your Spirit would move mightily, leading our nation into a new season where Your blessings overflow like dew from heaven. Let the barren places blossom; let joy spring up from the ashes. Raise up leaders and intercessors who will walk humbly with You, pursuing justice, mercy, and truth. Draw Your people close, united in purpose and love, as a bride adorned for her Bridegroom.

In this hour, we claim Your promises: "They shall come with weeping; they shall pray as I bring them back to their land." So we pray, Lord, bring Your people home—not only physically, but to the fullness of Your heart and destiny for this nation.

Turn our mourning into dancing. Replace despair with hope. Fill every broken place with Your joy and peace. May Your glory be revealed in the midst of us, and may this land be known as a nation under God, redeemed and renewed.

In Jesus' name, Amen.

Day 36: RESTORE US, AGAIN

For the Chief Musician. To the tune of "The Lily of the Covenant."
A teaching poem by David, when he fought with Aram
Naharaim and with Aram Zobah, and Joab returned, and killed
twelve thousand of Edom in the Valley of Salt. God, you have
rejected us. You have broken us down. You have been angry.
Restore us, again. You have made the land tremble. You have
torn it. Mend its fractures, for it quakes. You have shown your
people hard things. You have made us drink the wine that
makes us stagger. You have given a banner to those who fear
you, that it may be displayed because of the truth. Selah. So that
your beloved may be delivered, save with your right hand, and
answer us.
—Psalms 60:1-5 WEB

O God, You have rejected us, broken our defenses; You have been
angry—now restore us again. We cry out on behalf of this nation,
wounded by division, hardened by pride, and numbed by compromise.
You have made the land tremble; You have torn it open. Heal its
fractures, Lord, for it staggers. You alone are our Deliverer.

You have shown us hard things and given us wine that makes us stagger,
yet You also raise up a banner for those who fear You—a rallying point
in the storm. Today, we cling to that banner. We lift it high over our
homes, our courts, our churches, and our streets. Let it be a sign of Your
covenant mercy.

Stretch out Your right hand to save. Deliver us by Your mighty power.
Restore righteousness where injustice reigns. Revive reverence where
apathy has grown. Reform what is corrupt. Rebuild what is broken.
Reignite our destiny as a people who belong to You.

God of our fathers, do not cast us off forever. Hear the cries of those who still weep between the porch and the altar. Give us leaders after Your own heart. Give us mercy in the place of judgment. Give us You, Lord—more of You.

In Jesus' name, Amen.

Day 37: Revive Us Again

> Turn us, God of our salvation, and cause your indignation toward us to cease. Will you be angry with us forever? Will you draw out your anger to all generations? Won't you revive us again, that your people may rejoice in you? Show us your loving kindness, Yahweh. Grant us your salvation.
> —Psalms 85:4-7 WEB

Restore us again, O God of our salvation, and put away Your displeasure toward us. We come before You as those who mourn over the brokenness of our land—the divisions, the injustices, the pride, and the rebellion that have grieved Your heart. But still, You are merciful, and we believe You are not finished with us.

Will You be angry with us forever? Will Your wrath burn to all generations? No, Lord—we appeal to Your steadfast love. You are the same God who parted seas, who healed nations, who raised up prophets, and who poured out mercy on those who turned back to You. Do it again. Have mercy on us. Breathe life where apathy has reigned. Light a holy fire in the hearts of Your people. Let the winds of reformation blow through every system, every church, every family, and every heart.

Revive us, O God. Not just for comfort, but for purpose. Raise us up as a people marked by righteousness, humility, and holy boldness. Let Your glory dwell in our land again. Show us Your unfailing love, and grant us Your salvation—not only for ourselves, but for the generations to come.

In Jesus' name, Amen.

Day 38: DON'T CAST US OFF FOREVER

For the Lord will not cast off forever. For though he causes
grief, yet he will have compassion according to the multitude
of his loving kindnesses.
—Lamentations 3:31-32 WEB

Merciful Father,

Though we grieve over the sins of our land and the weight of judgment
we have brought upon ourselves, we hold fast to Your promise: *"For the
Lord will not cast off forever. But though He cause grief, yet He will have
compassion according to the multitude of His mercies."* We come boldly
before You—not in our righteousness, but in desperate need of Yours—
asking You to remember mercy in the midst of judgment.

Lord, we confess that our nation has wandered far. We've traded Your
truth for lies, Your righteousness for rebellion. But still, we stand in the
gap, pleading not for what we deserve, but for who You are—
compassionate, faithful, and abounding in steadfast love.

Do not cast us off forever. Heal the breaches in our land. Restore the
ruins of former generations. Rebuild the foundations of righteousness,
justice, and truth. Let Your mercy interrupt our cycles of sin and draw
us back to You in holy fear and humble surrender.

We believe You still have a purpose for this nation—a destiny to shine
as a beacon of Your glory. Revive us again, O Lord, that Your people may
rejoice in You. Let the weeping of this moment birth the reformation of
a generation.

In Jesus' name, Amen.

Day 39: DO A NEW THING, LORD

"Don't remember the former things, and don't consider the things of old. Behold, I will do a new thing. It springs out now. Don't you know it? I will even make a way in the wilderness, and rivers in the desert. The animals of the field shall honor me, the jackals and the ostriches; because I give water in the wilderness and rivers in the desert, to give drink to my people, my chosen, the people which I formed for myself, that they might declare my praise.
—Isaiah 43:18-21 WEB

Sovereign Lord, Holy One of Israel,

We come before You as intercessors for our nation—broken, weary, wandering—and we cry out: do a new thing in our land. You said, "Forget the former things; do not dwell on the past." And so, we release the weight of yesterday—every failure, every injustice, every idol we clung to instead of You. We let go of regret and remembrance that has become bondage, and we lift our eyes to behold the new thing You are doing, even now.

God of rivers in the wasteland, we ask You to break forth with streams of mercy across every dry and barren place in our nation. Let revival spring up where despair has ruled. Let unity rise where division has torn us apart. Make a way in the wilderness of our politics, our pulpits, our cities, and our homes.

You formed this people for Yourself, that we might declare Your praise. So raise up a remnant, Lord—those who will not bow to fear or pride, but who will walk in righteousness, reconciliation, and bold reformation. Awaken Your Church. Heal our land. Rewrite our national story in grace, truth, and glory. We believe, Lord. You are doing a new thing.

In Jesus' name, Amen.

Day 40: THERE SHALL BE SHOWERS OF BLESSING

> "'I will make with them a covenant of peace, and will cause evil animals to cease out of the land. They will dwell securely in the wilderness, and sleep in the woods. I will make them and the places around my hill a blessing. I will cause the shower to come down in its season. There will be showers of blessing. The tree of the field will yield its fruit, and the earth will yield its increase, and they will be secure in their land. Then they will know that I am Yahweh, when I have broken the bars of their yoke, and have delivered them out of the hand of those who made slaves of them. They will no more be a prey to the nations, neither will the animals of the earth devour them; but they will dwell securely, and no one will make them afraid.
> —Ezekiel 34:25-28 WEB

Sovereign Lord, our Covenant-Keeping Shepherd,

We come before You with hearts heavy for our land but full of hope in Your promises. You have said, *"I will make with them a covenant of peace and will cause the wild beasts to cease from the land, and they shall dwell safely in the wilderness and sleep in the woods."* So, we lift up our nation before You, pleading for Your divine peace to be restored within our borders—peace in our streets, peace in our homes, peace in our hearts.

Lord, we stand in the gap on behalf of the broken places. Where fear and violence have reigned, we call for Your covenant of peace to silence the wildness. Where the people have felt forsaken, we ask You to set them in safety. Let every desolate place be revived. Let every storm-ravaged soul find rest in Your covering.

You promised, *"I will cause showers to come down in their season; there shall be showers of blessing."* So, Father, we call for the rain—rain of Your mercy, rain of justice, rain of healing. Wash away our idols. Cleanse us of our pride. Soften the hardened places of this nation until the soil can once again receive Your Word with joy.

We decree over this land that we shall no longer be prey to the nations nor devoured by shame and division. You will break the yoke of bondage and rescue us from those who enslave. We ask for national reformation—not by the might of man, but by the Spirit of the Living God. Awaken us to righteousness. Restore us to covenant truth. Raise up leaders after Your heart. Heal our land according to Your promise.

Let the showers fall, Lord—not just a drizzle of revival but a downpour of transformation. Let this be the season when You visit us again with power, purpose, and peace.

In Jesus' name, Amen.

EPILOGUE

You've reached the end of the 40-day journey—but this is not the end of your assignment. If anything, it is just the beginning. Over these past days, you've cried out for peace, pleaded for truth, repented for a nation, and declared restoration over dry and broken places. Heaven has heard. Seeds have been sown. And now, we wait in faith for the harvest.

But don't stop here. The heart of an intercessor never clocks out. Stay on the wall. Keep listening, keep praying, and keep standing in the gap. God is not finished with your nation. His plans are greater than what we see, and His promises are still true. As you move forward, carry the burden with hope, knowing that your prayers are part of a bigger story—a story of redemption, reformation, and revival that only God can write.

May your life be a lighthouse of truth. May your voice echo the heart of heaven. And may you never forget: one person praying in the will of God can shape the destiny of a nation.

Keep standing. Keep believing. God is healing the land.

What Happens Next?

1. **Keep Praying.**
   Revisit these prayers as needed. Use them during election cycles, national days of mourning or celebration, or when the news headlines grow heavy. Prayer is not seasonal—it is eternal.

2. **Go Deeper.**

   Let this spark fuel a lifestyle of watchfulness. Begin to pray for your local leaders, school boards, police, churches, and neighborhoods. God is not only concerned with nations—He's concerned with every person who lives in them.

3. **Mobilize Others.**

   Start a prayer group. Share what you've learned. Invite your church, youth ministry, or Bible study into this mission. Prayer is contagious—and right now, our nation needs an outbreak of it.

4. **Trust God's Timing.**

   Not every answer will come immediately, and not every shift will be visible. But the Word is clear: *"The prayer of a righteous person is powerful and effective"* (James 5:16). God is working—even in silence.

A Final Word of Hope

Remember, the battle for a nation is won first and foremost in the realm of prayer and spiritual surrender. Your prayers have not been in vain.

Keep this flame of intercession burning in your heart beyond these pages. Let it ignite a lifelong commitment to seek God's will for your nation, your community, and your own life. Trust that the God who commands the heavens and the earth is also guiding the steps of those who place their hope in Him.

May you continue to be a watchman on the walls, a voice for justice, and a bearer of peace. And may the nation whose God is the Lord be blessed now and forevermore.

In Jesus' name, Amen.

Encourage Others with Your Story

If this prayer guide has strengthened your faith, deepened your intercession, or helped you stand in the gap for our nation, would you consider leaving a short review on Amazon? Your feedback not only encourages others but also helps more believers discover this resource and join in praying for this nation. Every review—just a few sentences—makes a difference and helps spread the call to stand in the gap. Thank you for being part of this movement.

MORE FROM PRAYERSCRIPTS

STANDING IN THE GAP FOR COVENANT AWAKENING:

30 DAYS OF PRAYER FOR NATIONAL REPENTANCE, RIGHTEOUS LEADERSHIP & GOD'S SOVEREIGN RULE

What if your prayers could help turn the tide of a nation?

America stands at a spiritual crossroads. Division deepens, truth is under siege, and righteousness is being redefined. But God is still searching for those who will stand in the gap—intercessors who will cry out for mercy, justice, and national awakening.

Standing in the Gap for Covenant Awakening is a 30-day prayer guide for believers who sense the urgency of the hour and long to see their nation return to God.

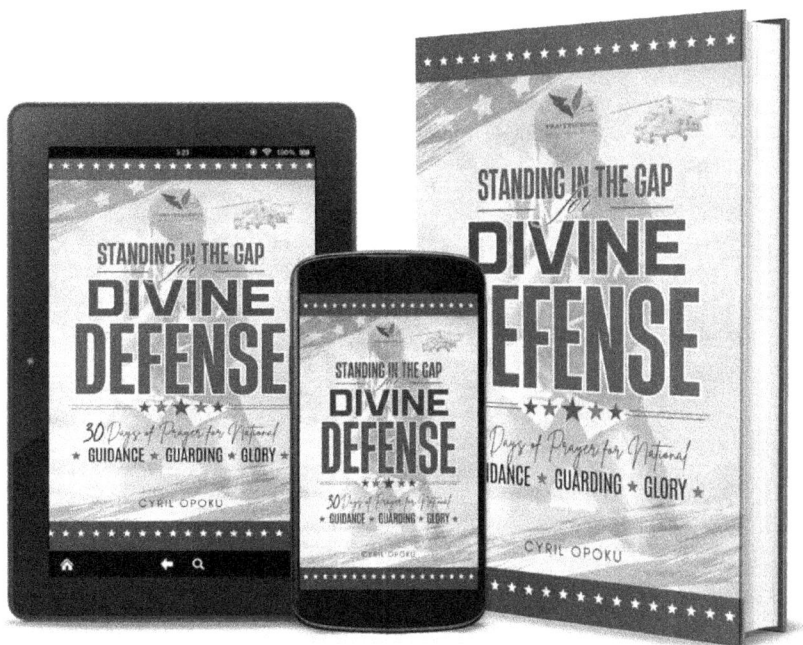

STANDING IN THE GAP FOR DIVINE DEFENSE:

30 DAYS OF PRAYER FOR NATIONAL GUIDANCE, GUARDING & GLORY

When the foundations of a nation feel as if they're shaking, prayer is the strongest fortress you can build.

Standing in the Gap for Divine Defense: 30 Days of Prayer for National Guidance, Guarding & Glory is your call to action—a 30-day journey of powerful, Scripture-rooted intercession that invites everyday believers to become watchmen on the walls for their nation. Drawing on timeless truths from God's Word, this devotional equips you to stand in the gap for your nation and **Seek Heaven's Wisdom, Secure Divine Protection,** and **Ignite Spiritual Awakening.** If you sense the urgency of the hour and long to see your country guided and guarded by the hand of God, open these pages. Stand in the gap. Watch Him move.

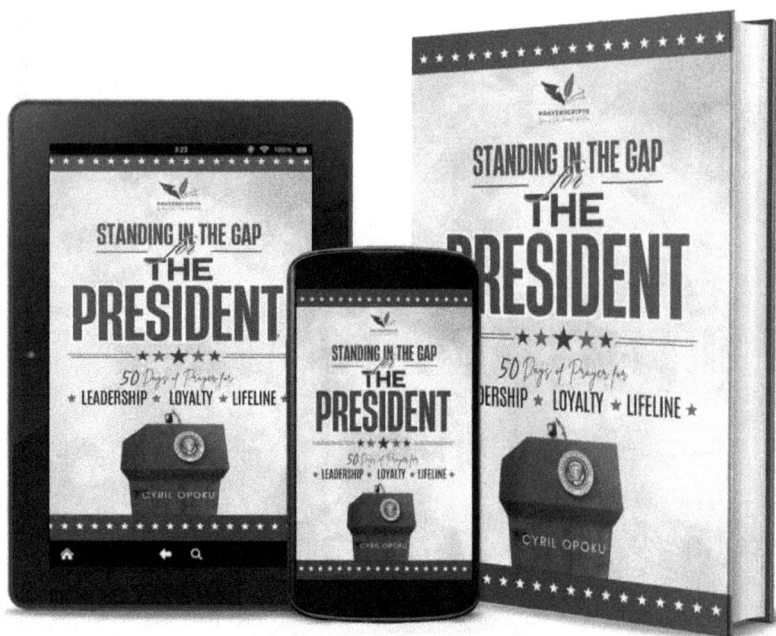

STANDING IN THE GAP FOR THE PRESIDENT:

50 DAYS OF PRAYER FOR LEADERSHIP, LOYALTY, AND LIFELINE

When a nation's leader is under spiritual siege, will you answer the call to stand in the gap?

Standing in the Gap for The President: 50 Days of Prayer for Leadership, Loyalty, and Lifeline is a bold, Scripture-saturated prayer guide for those who understand that the battles facing our leaders are more than political—they are spiritual. Assassination attempts, betrayal from within, and attacks on character and conscience are not just headlines—they're signs of the times. Inside, you'll find 50 days of strategic intercession divided into three high-impact sections: **Presidential Character & Leadership, Against Disloyal Insiders**, and **Against Assassination Attempts.** The future of a nation can shift through the prayers of the faithful. It's time to stand in the gap.

SCRIPTURES & PRAYERS FOR DELIVERANCE FROM TROUBLE:
40 DAYS OF PRAYER FOR WHEN LIFE FEELS OVERWHELMING

Are you walking through a season where life feels heavy, hope feels distant, and your prayers feel weak?

Scriptures & Prayers for Deliverance from Trouble is a 40-day journey of honest prayers and powerful Scriptures to help you find peace, strength, and healing when life is overwhelming. Each day offers a personal, Scripture-based prayer written in the language of real faith and raw trust. This devotional isn't about perfect words—it's about real connection with God when you need Him most.

Scriptures & Prayers for Deliverance from Evil:
50 Days of Prayer to Overcome Darkness and Find God's Protection

When darkness presses in, how do you pray?

When fear grips your heart or unseen battles rage around you, you need more than generic words—you need Scripture, truth, and the steady hand of God to lead you through.

Scriptures & Prayers for Deliverance from Evil: 50 Days of Prayer to Overcome Darkness and Find God's Protection is a powerful devotional journey designed to help you pray boldly and biblically through seasons of spiritual warfare, oppression, fear, or uncertainty.

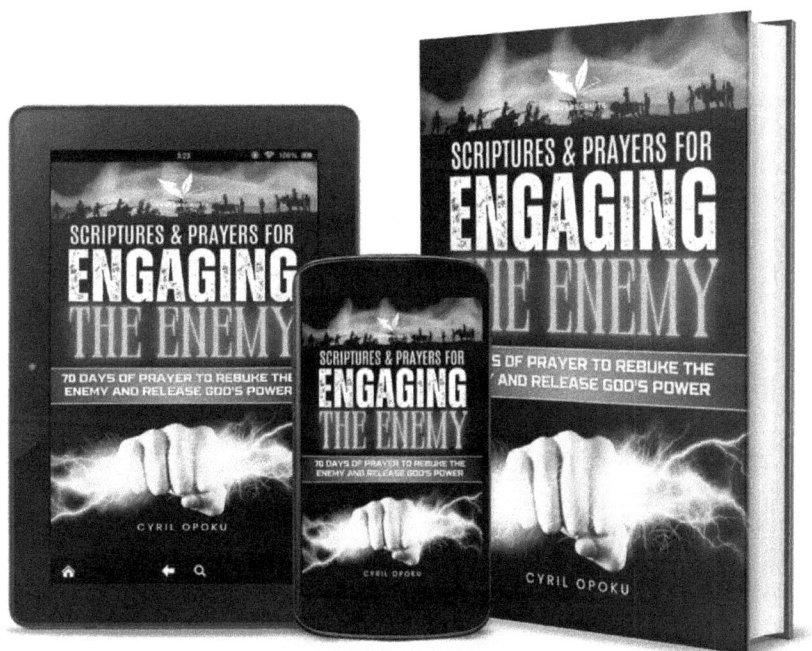

SCRIPTURES & PRAYERS FOR ENGAGING THE ENEMY:
70 DAYS OF PRAYER TO REBUKE THE ENEMY AND RELEASE GOD'S POWER

You weren't called to run from the battle—
you were anointed to win it.

Scriptures & Prayers for Engaging the Enemy: 70 Days of Prayer to Rebuke the Enemy and Release God's Power is a bold devotional for believers who are ready to rise, resist, and reclaim what the enemy has tried to steal. If you're tired of feeling spiritually outnumbered, this book will equip you to fight back—with Scripture in your mouth and power in your prayers. Over 70 days, you'll be guided through five strategic phases of spiritual warfare: (1) Rebuking the Enemy, (2) Releasing Terror Upon the Enemy (3) Praying for the Fall of the Enemy (4) Treading Upon the Enemy (5) When Heaven Strikes.

The war is real. But so is your victory.

SCRIPTURES & PRAYERS FOR COMBATING SPIRITUAL WICKEDNESS:
50 DAYS OF PRAYER TO OVERTHROW WICKED PLANS AND STAND IN GOD'S VICTORY

Are you facing opposition that feels deeper than the natural? Do you sense hidden resistance working against your progress, peace, or purpose? You're not imagining it—and you're not powerless.

Rooted in the authority of Scripture and fueled by bold, targeted prayers, *Scriptures & Prayers for Combating Spiritual Wickedness* equips you to confront darkness head-on. Each day features a focused Bible passage and a heartfelt, Scripture-based prayer designed to nullify ungodly counsel, disrupt demonic schemes, and establish God's victory in every area of your life.

www.ingramcontent.com/pod-product-compliance
Lightning Source LLC
Chambersburg PA
CBHW060401050426
42449CB00009B/1854